Birth of Toads

Birth of Toads

Elvig Hansen

Translated by Noel Simon

J.M. Dent & Sons Ltd
London & Melbourne

First published in Great Britain 1986
English translation © J.M. Dent & Sons Ltd 1985
Originally published in German under the title
Aus dem Leben der Erdkröte
© Kinderbuchverlag KBV Luzern AG 1985
All rights reserved

Printed in Germany
This book is set in Itek Century Schoolbook
by Copyright, London W1

British Library Cataloguing in Publication Data
Hansen, Elvig
 Birth of toads.
 1. Frogs—Juvenile literature 2. Toads—
Juvenile literature
 I. Title II. Aus dem Leben der Erdkröte. *English*
 597.8 QL668.E2
 ISBN 0-460-06226-3

Altogether there are about 240 species of toads in the world. The one which is the subject of this book is the most common European species. Toads, like their relatives the frogs, belong to a very ancient class of animals, the amphibians. For many millions of years animals lived only in water. The amphibians were the first group of vertebrate animals to move on to land.

The toad's life begins in water. That is where it lays its eggs. After the eggs have hatched the young spend the first few weeks of their lives in the water as tadpoles. After two or three months, during which time the tadpoles develop into tiny toads, they move to the land, where they remain for the rest of their lives – except for a fortnight each year when they return to ponds, pools, streams or marshes to mate and lay their eggs.

Toads are active mainly at night; by day they conceal themselves in dark, moist hiding places. This helps to explain why in olden times people associated them with witchcraft. The poison which the toad secretes was used in a variety of charms and spells, and sometimes for medicinal purposes. Toads have long been regarded as ugly, sinister and dangerous creatures. We now know that they are not only completely harmless but even useful. They kill snakes and many other garden pests.

But despite a greater understanding of toads, they are having increasing difficulty in surviving in Europe under modern conditions. During the course of their spring migration, huge numbers of toads are run over on the roads. More and more ponds, and other wetlands — the toads' breeding grounds — are disappearing, often through being filled in or used as refuse dumps. The toad is also endangered by people spraying their gardens and fields with poisonous insecticides. Sprays kill many insects, including those on which the toad feeds. Where conditions are unspoiled, toads can be expected to live for a long time, from ten to twenty years. One toad is known to have lived in captivity for about thirty-six years. But nowadays few toads survive more than one or two years in the wild state, and, out of every 2,000 to 3,000 tadpoles, only a single one may succeed in developing into an adult toad.

This book enables you to see how a toad is born and how it manages to survive and develop. It also shows how the adult toad lives: from spring when it awakes from its winter sleep through to early winter when it is time once again to hibernate.

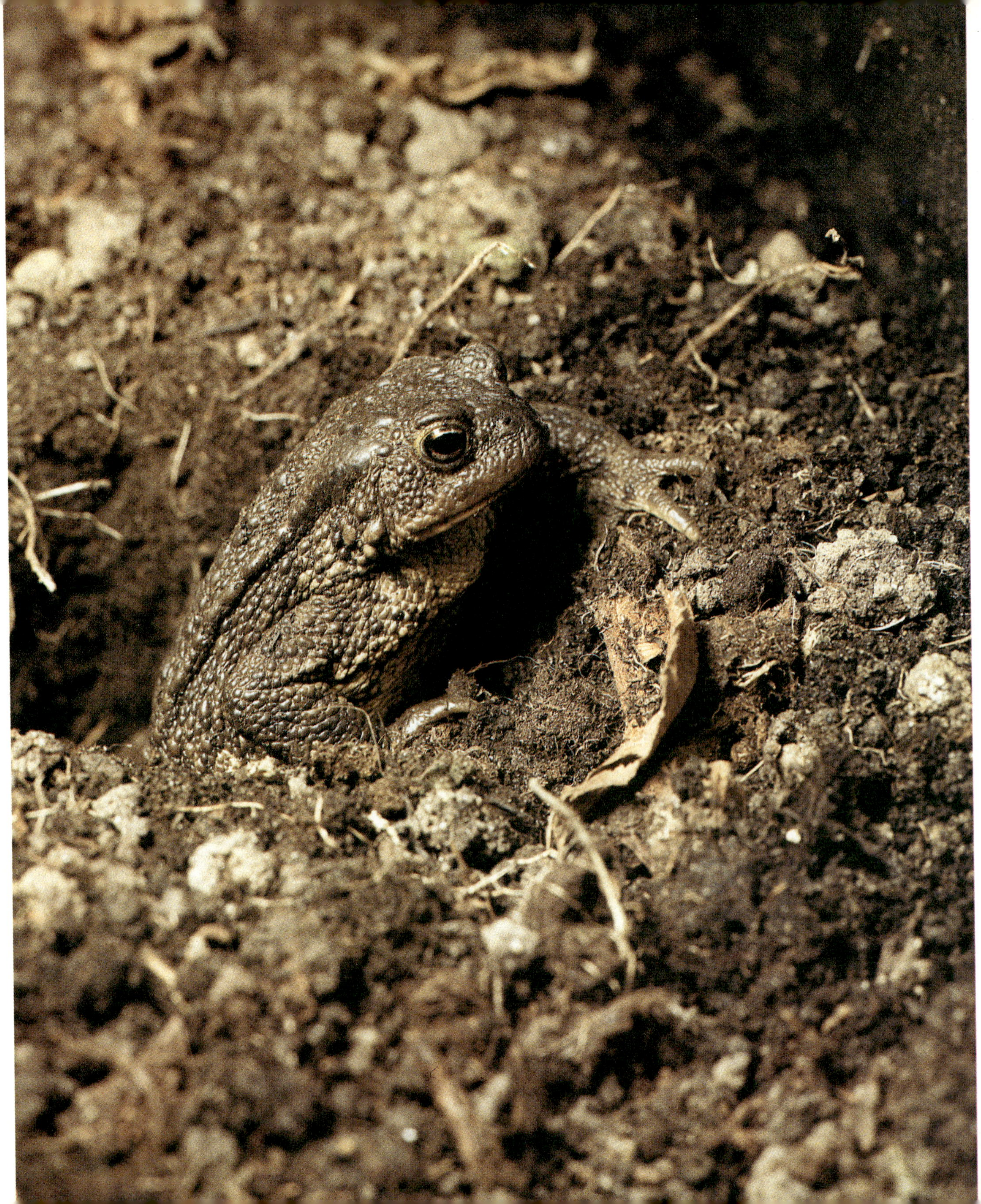

Spring is a time when nature is intensely active. Plants burst into life, and animals emerge from their hiding places after sleeping all winter.

One day early in April, when standing in our greenhouse, I noticed the earth in one of the corners suddenly move: a toad was digging its way out of the ground. The next day, as I was shifting a pile of firewood, I found a second toad fast asleep under the wood stack.

Toads spend the winter in a variety of places, very often in the woodlands where they occupy hollows in the ground filled with piles of leaves. There they are protected from the frost which they cannot tolerate. These two toads moved in to an unoccupied mousehole for the winter. They slept soundly, without a care in the world!

On waking from their long winter sleep the toads at once start to migrate. At dusk, and during the night, they crawl through gardens, across fields or over roads and highways. And there, on the roads, their wandering often comes to an abrupt end. One evening we counted eight toads that had been run over on our small road.

You may well wonder why toads have such an urge to wander. There is nothing to stop them remaining wherever they happen to have spent the winter. Then they would not run the risk of being killed by cars. But toads have an instinctive and compulsive urge to migrate. It is vital for them to find a pond or pool in which to lay their eggs.

A number of toads have gathered near a pond. Some of the smaller toads are mounted on the backs of the larger – as if exhausted after their long migration. The smaller toads are the males. They are only about 8 cm long. The females are almost twice as large, growing up to 13 cm.

On the right is a mass of toads. No less than nine males are struggling to mount a single female to mate with her.

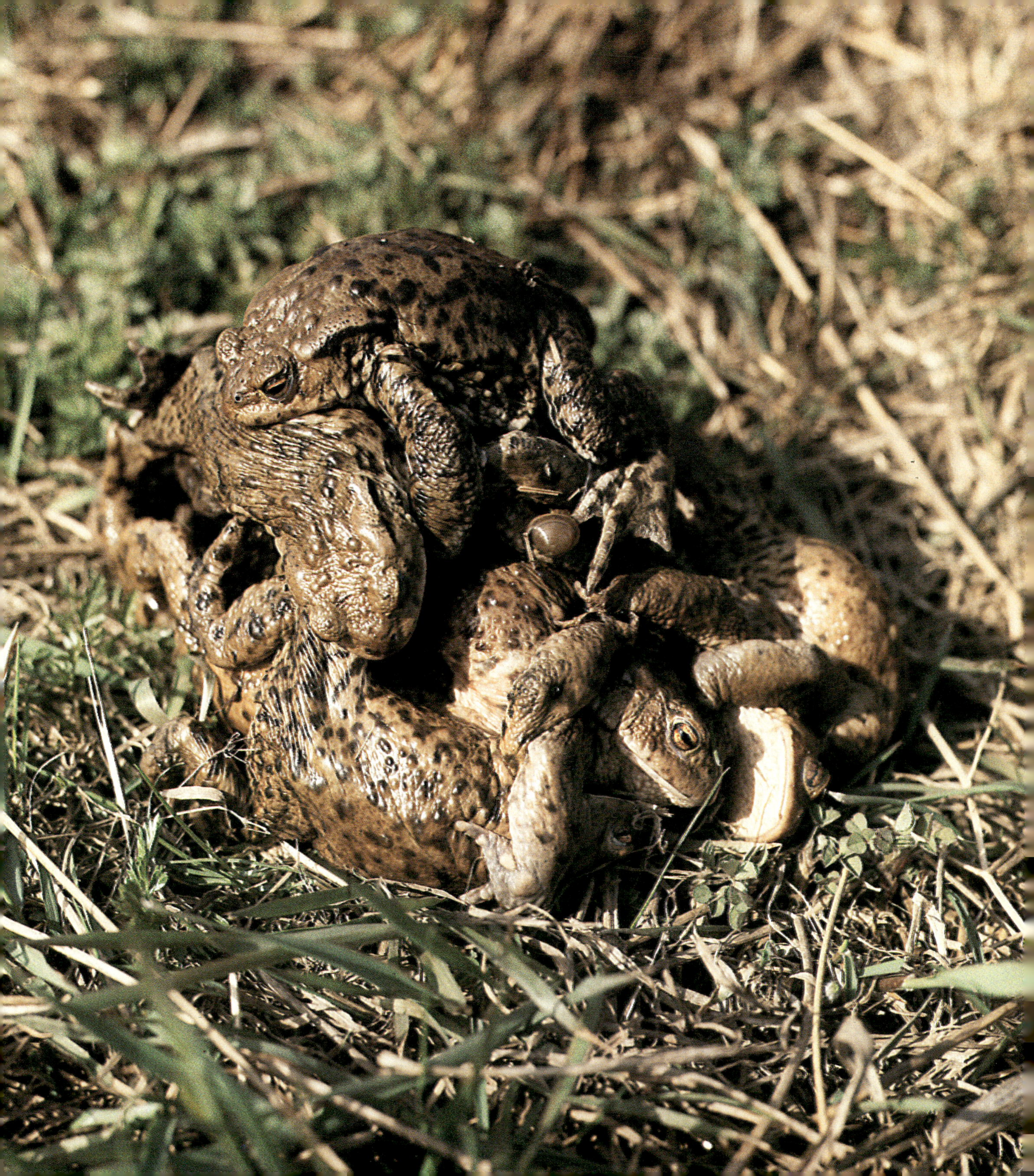

More and more toads converge on the pool. They are very timid. The moment we disturb them they submerge beneath the water. Males which have not yet found a female continue to search for a mate. When one male spots another close by, it lets out a croaking noise which sounds rather like a cough or a bark. This mating call attracts the females, and at the same time warns other males off. Male toads try to mate with almost anything that happens to be in the water which even remotely resembles a female. Indeed, the male in this picture is trying to mount an old tin can!

Sitting on the edge of the pool I gently stir the water with my gumboots. Almost at once a male toad swims straight towards me and clasps the toe of my boot. He evidently mistakes it for a rather outsize female!

Other males have better luck in finding females. The number of pairs in the water is increasing all the time, but only their heads are visible above the surface.

During mating the male toad clings tightly to the female's back, grasping her with his forelegs. Little horny pads on the first three fingers help him to grip tightly.

The female now lays her eggs – known as toads' spawn. The eggs appear in the form of two long chains of jelly, rather like strings of beads, which become coiled around the stems of water plants. Each 'string' is the thickness of two or three eggs, and many hundreds in length.

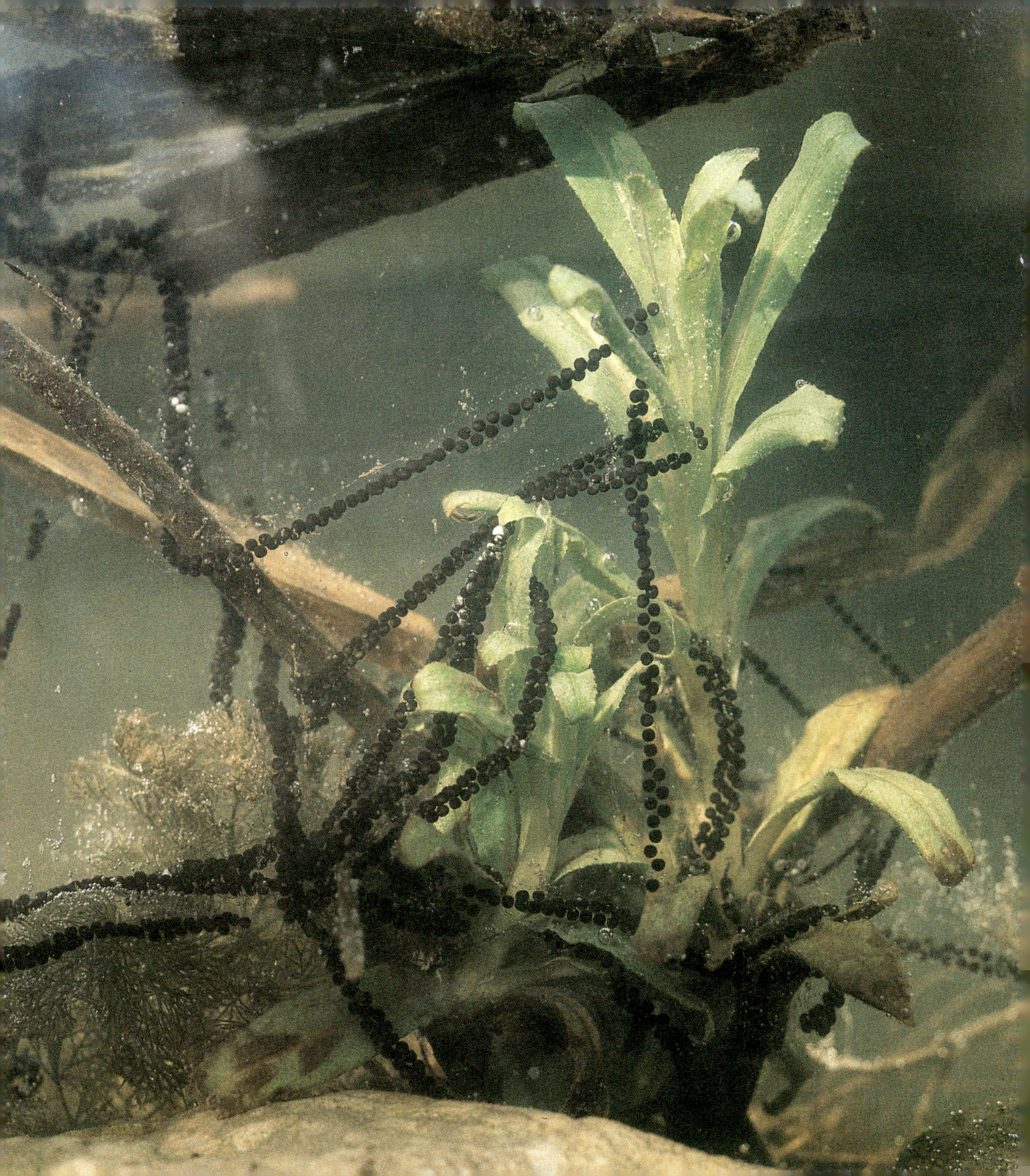

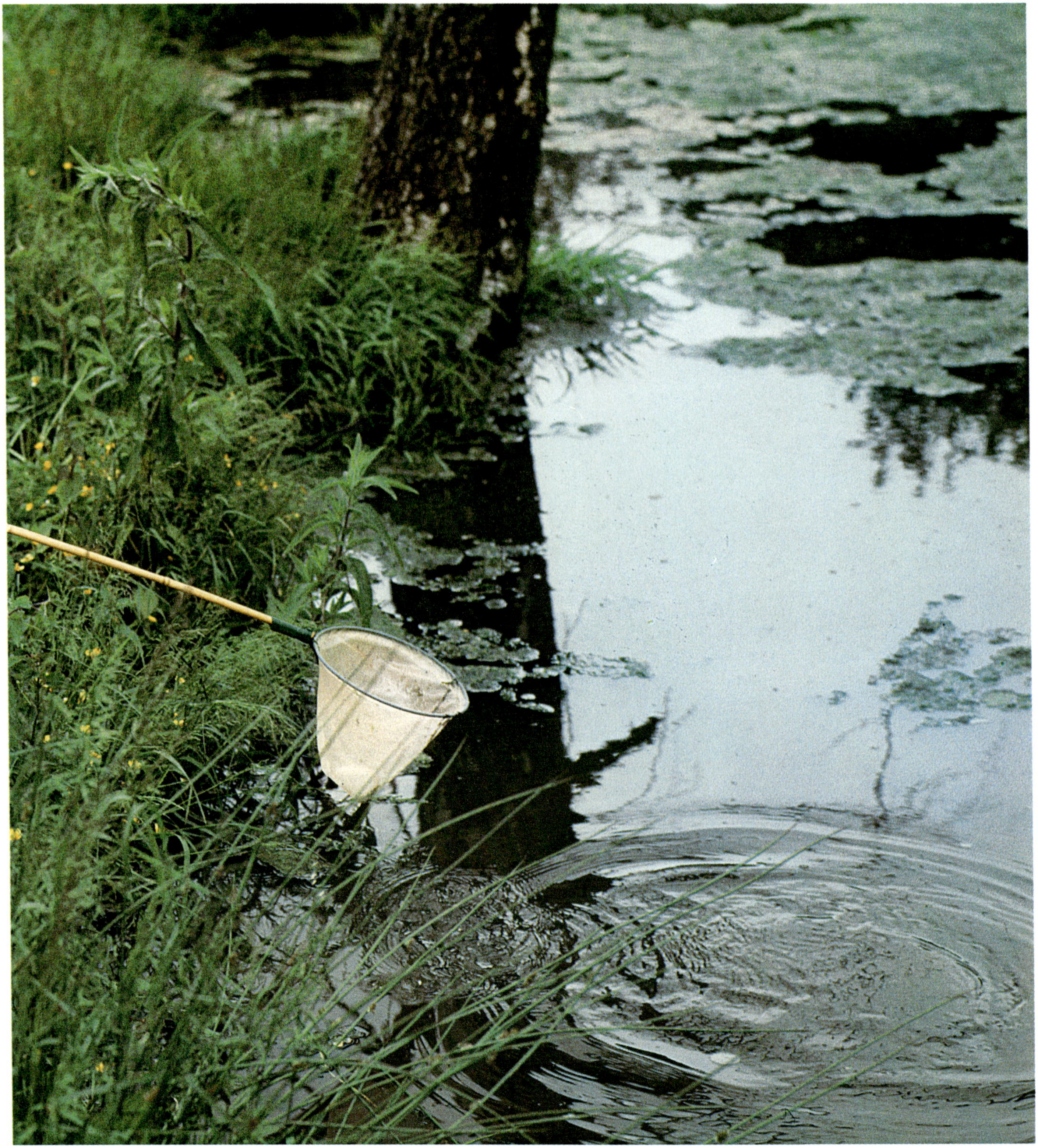

As the female lays her eggs – approximately 6,000 of them – the male releases his sperm over them. That is how the eggs are fertilized. After that the parent toads move away from the pond, leaving the eggs unprotected.

After eight days the tadpoles emerge from the eggs. For the first few days of their lives they spend their time either perching on the stems of pond plants or swimming about. Some of these little tadpoles are brought to the surface in the net we use for catching sticklebacks. But we immediately throw them back into the water.

The newborn tadpoles are only 7 or 8 mm long. They grow rapidly, however. One month later they will have doubled in size – if the tail is included. They breathe with the aid of gills, like fish, but have only one gill opening. The tadpoles in our pond have plenty of algae to eat. Algae are tiny plants which grow on larger plants or stones. The tadpoles scrape off the algae with their horny snouts. But they also eat carrion – dead animals. The one in the photograph below is a dead leech.

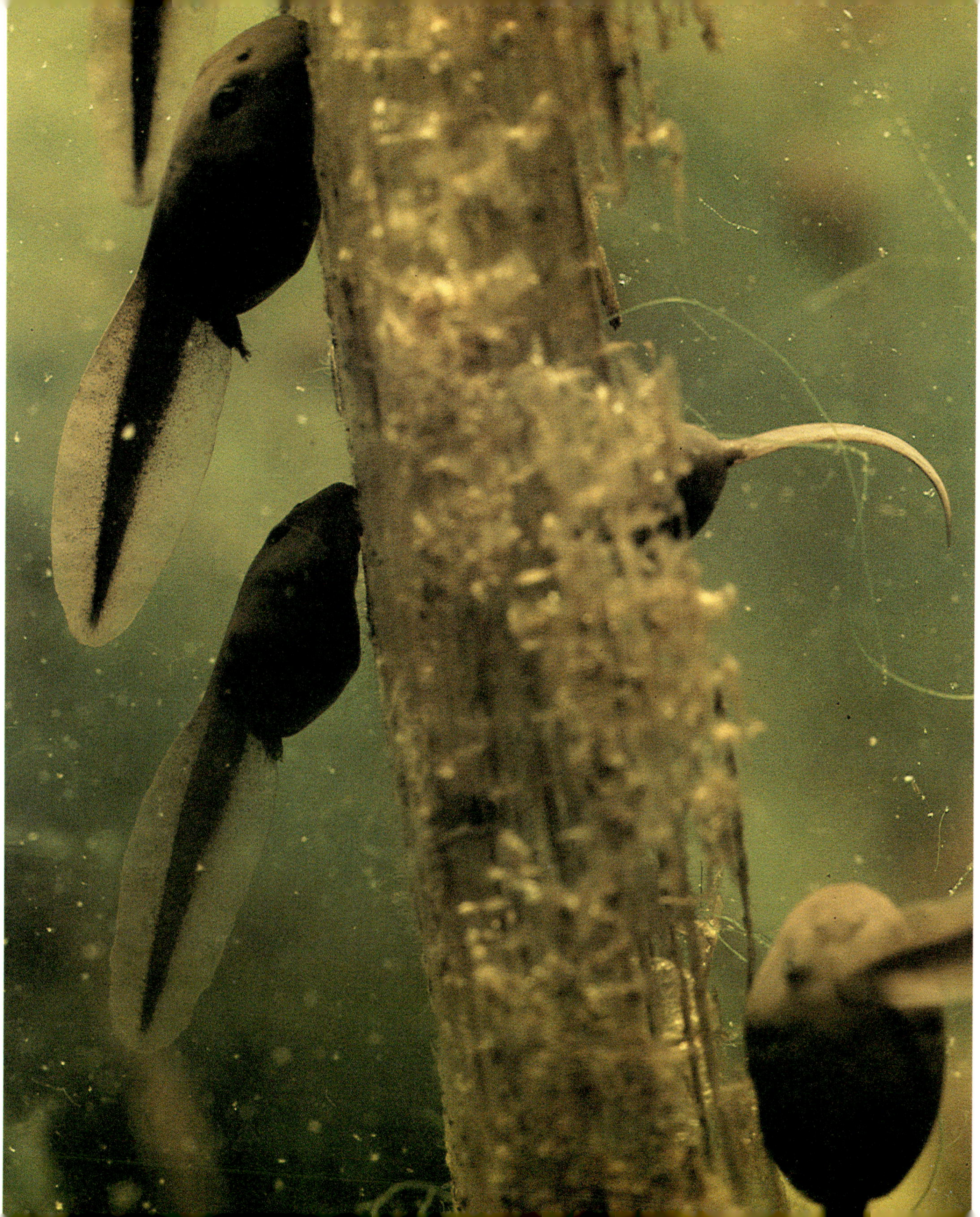

As long as there is plenty to eat the tadpoles grow quickly. During the summer an interesting change takes place. Tadpoles are designed to live in water, whereas when they become toads they live on land. But before they can move from water to land their bodies have to change to suit their new way of life.

First, two bulges appear, one on either side of the tail; they become longer and longer. By the time the tadpole is about six weeks old these two projections can be recognized as a pair of long hindlegs, each of which has five toes. The forelegs follow at the age of about eight weeks, although they have only four 'fingers' apiece. The tadpole now has four legs and a tail, and looks like a four-footed animal.

Four days later the tail has practically disappeared. The gills, through which the tadpole breathes, have also vanished: their function is taken over by lungs. Within two to three months the tadpole has changed into a fully-formed toad. The picture on the right shows small toadlets perching on the stem of a plant on the surface of the pond, breathing through their lungs.

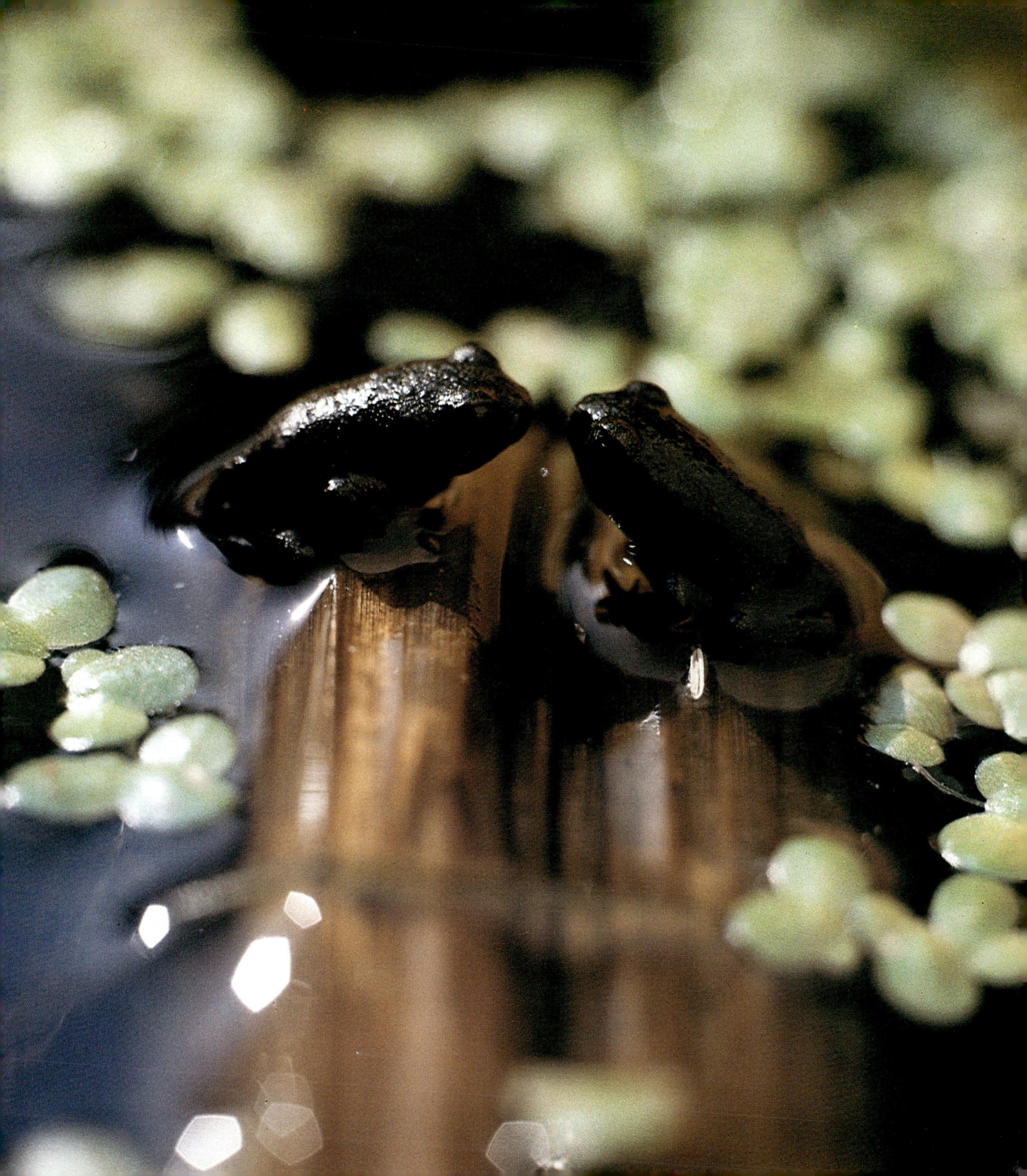

Two days later we can hardly believe our eyes. Masses of small black dots are crawling and hopping about. They seem to be everywhere – on plants, on rocks, on the land, and on the green duckweed floating on the surface of the water. The many hundreds, perhaps even thousands, of little black dots are toadlets! They are all leaving the water and making their way to the land. It is essential for the toadlet to reach dry land or they will drown. Now that they breathe through lungs it is impossible for them to remain any longer under water.

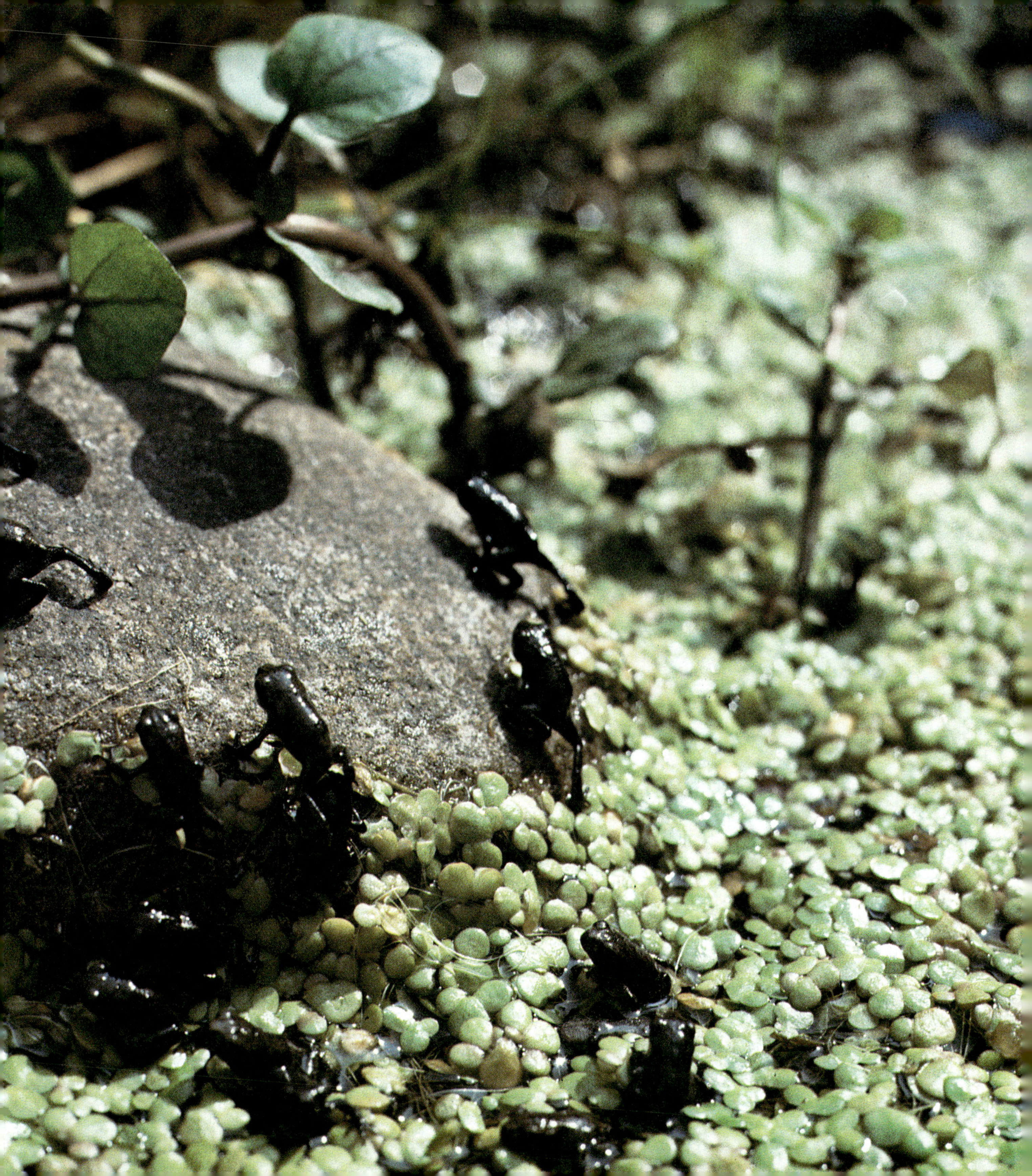

The toadlets are so small – only 8-10 mm long – that they are extremely difficult to see. The picture below shows one of them sitting close to a ladybird; the two are about the same size. The toadlet in the picture on the right has seen something that alarms it, something that moves very slowly. The toadlet remains quite still, staring at the strange animal. It must seem very large: in fact, this slug is only 2 cm long.

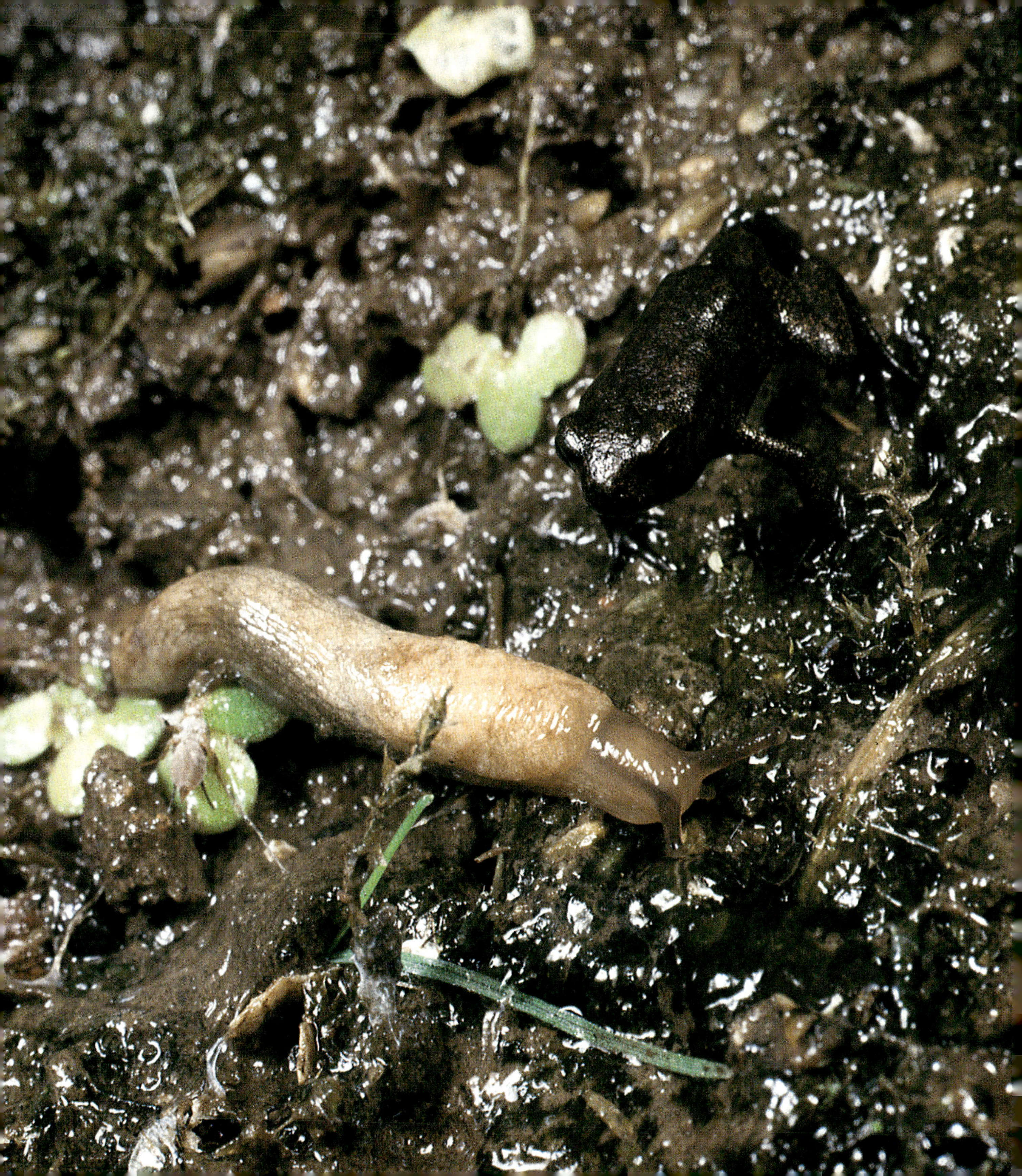

The toadlets do not eat algae. Their horny snouts have disappeared. These have been replaced by long, sticky tongues with which to catch prey – animals which are no bigger than 1 mm. These small creatures exist in huge numbers. In the grass around the pond are hordes of greenflies. When the wind ripples the grass, many greenflies fall to the ground where the toadlets lie in wait. Once a toadlet has found a greenfly it crawls quite slowly up to it. Stiff-legged, it draws close. When it is about 4 mm from the greenfly it pauses.

For a few seconds the toadlet stands staring at its prey. Suddenly, its long tongue shoots out of its mouth like a lasso, grabbing the greenfly at lightning speed and gobbling it up. The toadlet remains still, swallowing a few times, before continuing the hunt.

Four or five greenflies are enough to satisfy the toadlet's appetite. Finding a suitable place among the blades of grass, it settles down to rest and digest its meal.

Some days after the toadlets have moved on to the land they, too, migrate. They roam in their thousands over fields and roads, large numbers of them inevitably being killed. But when the instinctive urge to reach their summer quarters is upon them they react in the same way as the adults. Not until they are four years old, by which time they are fully grown, do they return to the pond in which they were born in order to breed.

Below, you can see a toadlet, only eight days old, and an adult of about four years. How small the toadlet seems in comparison with the adult! Five toadlets together weigh only 1 gram, whereas a full-grown toad weighs about 80 grams. It is easy to see how simple it would be for the adults to attack the smaller ones and devour them. Many toads try to do so, but they don't, in fact, like the taste. Toads protect themselves from their enemies by exuding a substance from their poison glands which has an unpleasant smell and taste.

Toads have no teeth. They cannot therefore chew. Instead, they have to swallow their prey whole. The larger the toad, the larger the animals it can devour. A full-grown toad can easily swallow a thick earthworm. After first watching the worm as it moves, the toad hops a step nearer. Stiff-legged, with body raised and head bent forward, it stands close to the worm, staring at it intently. Then – quick as a flash – the long, sticky tongue suddenly shoots out.

Seizing the worm with its tongue the toad draws it into its mouth. Before swallowing the worm, the toad pins it against the ground with its forelegs. Whenever the toad swallows, it closes its eyes. It has to swallow again and again in order to get the large earthworm down its throat and into its stomach. The worm tries to escape but has no chance of doing so. Finally, the toad closes its mouth firmly – and that is the end of the worm. The entire incident takes only a couple of minutes.

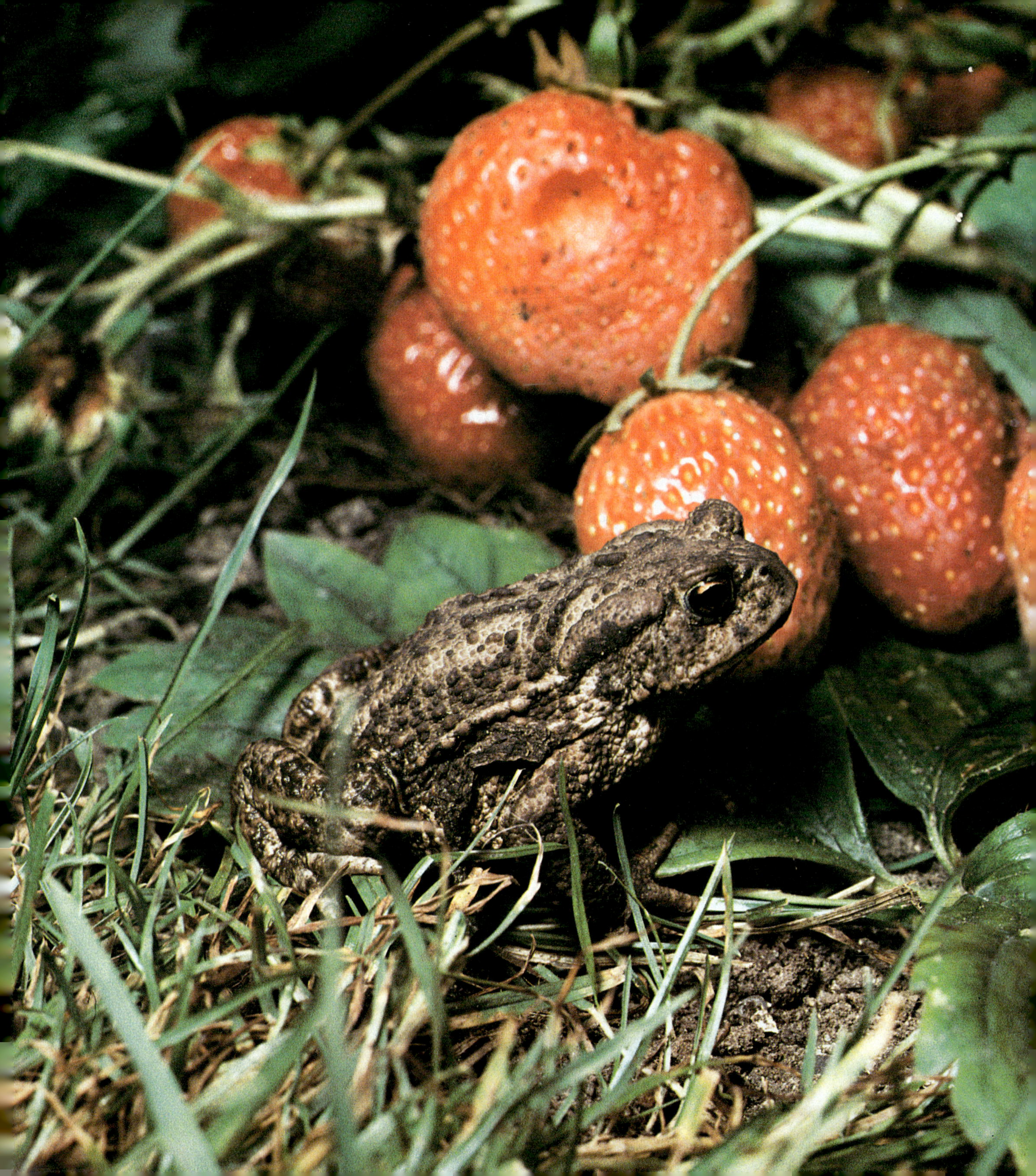

For several days we have been watching a toad in a bed of ripe strawberries. You may think the toad is eating the strawberries. But it is not. All toads are carnivorous. They never eat plants or fruit – not even strawberries, however delectable they may seem to us. A toad visits a strawberry bed only to hunt for slugs. Many gardeners are delighted to have toads in their vegetable gardens or greenhouses. They consume huge numbers of slugs and insects which would otherwise harm valuable plants.

Do cats eat toads? No, toads do not taste good, as you already know. Cats merely play with toads, as they do, for instance, with shrews, which they do not eat either. When a toad is attacked it raises itself on all four legs. At the same time it blows itself up to give the impression of being larger than it really is. This helps to scare off its attacker. Moreover, behind the eyes are two large glands which secrete an acrid and poisonous fluid. That is sufficient to deter most enemies. Indeed, although snakes, hedgehogs, weasels and storks frequently attack toads, they seldom actually eat them.

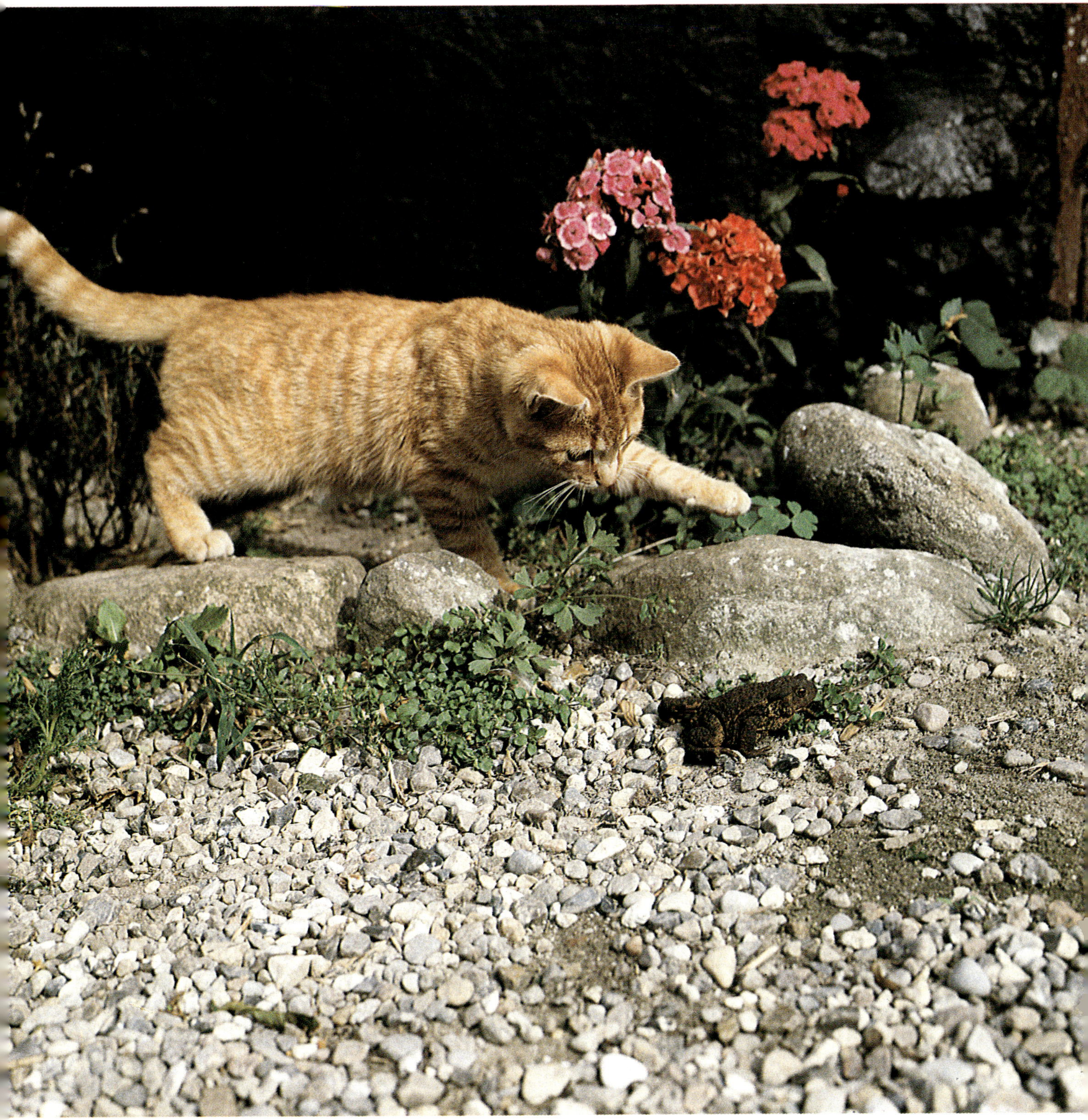

Toads can be found in all sorts of places, including dark cellars. Two large toads have lived in our cellar for several years. After the breeding migration, they have always returned to us. But what can toads possibly find to eat in a cellar? There are certainly no earthworms or slugs. On the other hand, a damp cellar houses plenty of woodlice, millipedes, spiders and other insects – all delicacies for toads.

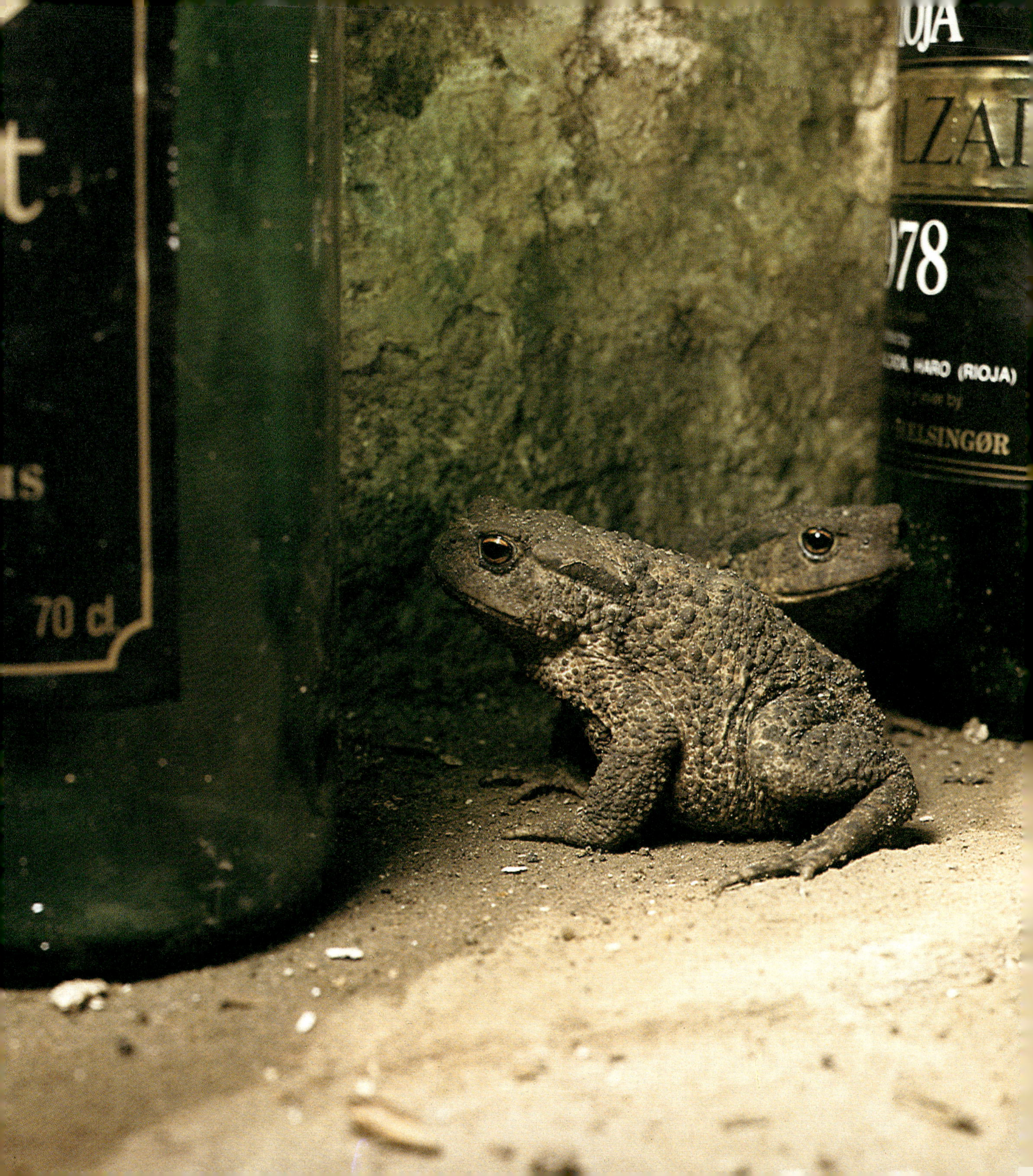
70 cl
HARO (RIOJA)

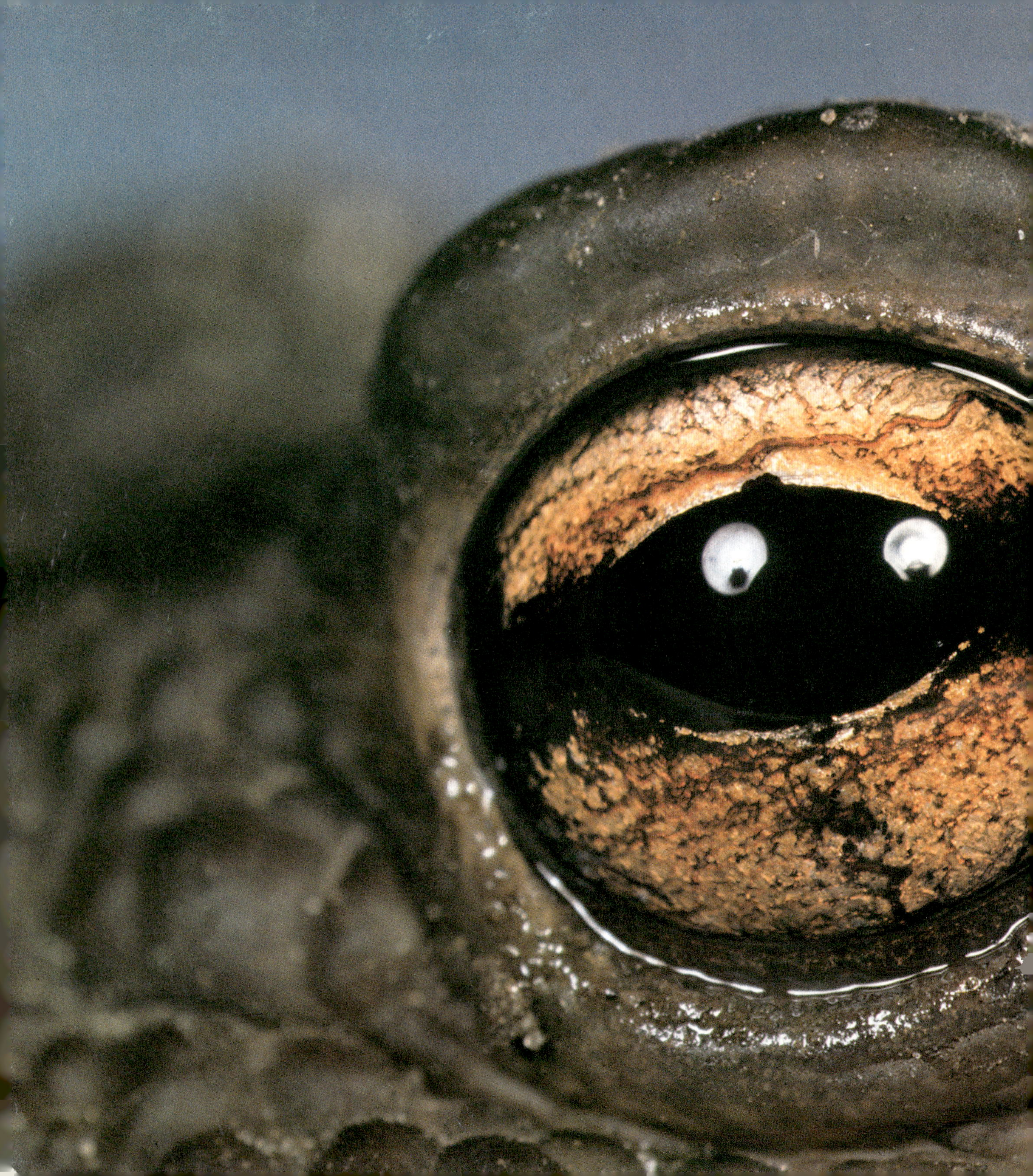

The picture above is a close-up of the toad's rough and bumpy skin, and shows quite clearly how thickly it is covered with warts. But as for the toad's eyes, I find them almost jewel-like, the gold-coloured irises being particularly beautiful.

After you have handled a toad you must always be sure to wash your hands thoroughly in case a trace of poison remains. If you were to lick your fingers, the venom could get into your stomach and cause you to become ill. But it is not dangerous.

Autumn has come round once more and it is already quite cold outside. One evening I see a toad crawling around our greenhouse. At last it finds a spot where the soil is soft. Using its hindlegs, the toad scoops out the soil, and pushes its hindquarters downwards. At the same hindquarters downwards. At the same time it shoves the loose earth which it has scraped from the sides of the burrow out of the way. Backing into the hole, the toad works its way deeper and deeper into the ground. At a depth of about 20 cm it turns around. It then pulls in earth from above, thus filling in the hole and burying itself completely.

Until the coming of spring, the toad remains in its winter quarters. Then, in March or April, it emerges and at once moves down to the pond, there to breed. And so the cycle begins anew.

Conservationists and naturalists must ensure that as many toads as possible – and also frogs – are given the chance to reach their breeding ponds without being run over on the way. Closing sections of certain roads along their migration routes, for example, or laying pipes under the roads, would be a real help. They soon learn to use these underpasses. Only when people take the trouble to look after them will these animals survive.